Comparison of Limnological Characteristics and Distribution and Abundance of Littoral Macroinvertebrates and Zooplankton in Fish-bearing and Fishless Lakes of Lassen Volcanic National Park

Natural Resource Technical Report NPS/KLMN/NRTR—2008/116

Michael S. Parker
Department of Biology
Southern Oregon University
Ashland, OR 97520

August 2008

U.S. Department of the Interior
National Park Service
Natural Resource Program Center
Fort Collins, Colorado

The Natural Resource Publication series addresses natural resource topics that are of interest and applicability to a broad readership in the National Park Service and to others in the management of natural resources, including the scientific community, the public, and the NPS conservation and environmental constituencies. Manuscripts are peer-reviewed to ensure that the information is scientifically credible, technically accurate, appropriately written for the intended audience, and is designed and published in a professional manner.

The Natural Resources Technical Reports series is used to disseminate the peer-reviewed results of scientific studies in the physical, biological, and social sciences for both the advancement of science and the achievement of the National Park Service's mission. The reports provide contributors with a forum for displaying comprehensive data that are often deleted from journals because of page limitations. Current examples of such reports include the results of research that addresses natural resource management issues; natural resource inventory and monitoring activities; resource assessment reports; scientific literature reviews; and peer reviewed proceedings of technical workshops, conferences, or symposia.

Views, statements, findings, conclusions, recommendations and data in this report are solely those of the author(s) and do not necessarily reflect views and policies of the U.S. Department of the Interior, NPS. Mention of trade names or commercial products does not constitute endorsement or recommendation for use by the National Park Service.

Printed copies of reports in these series may be produced in a limited quantity and they are only available as long as the supply lasts. This report is also available from the Natural Resource Publications Management website (http://www.nature.nps.gov/publications/NRPM) on the Internet or by sending a request to the address on the back cover.

This report is also available from the Klamath I&M Network website at (http://www.nature.nps.gov/im/units/KLMN).

Please cite this publication as:

Parker, M. S. 2008. Comparison of limnological characteristics and distribution and abundance of littoral macroinvertebrates and zooplankton in fish-bearing and fishless lakes of Lassen Volcanic National Park. Natural Resource Technical Report NPS/KLMN/NRTR—2008/116. National Park Service, Fort Collins, Colorado.

NPS D-164, August 2008

Contents

Tables

Figures

Abstract

The stocking of non-native fishes into lakes of Lassen Volcanic National Park (LVNP) was discontinued in the late 1970s and many lakes have since returned to a fishless condition. Due to a lack of comprehensive surveys, however, present fish distributions were largely unknown as were impacts of fish predation on native biota. Here we present results of a study examining the distribution of introduced fishes and their ongoing effects on littoral macroinvertebrate and zooplankton assemblages among larger (>2 m deep), natural lakes and ponds likely to have been stocked in the past. In a companion study, Stead et al. (2005) presented results of the first comprehensive survey of fish and amphibian distributions among all lentic habitats within LVNP. Of 73 natural lakes and ponds examined in this study, 10 (13.7%) supported fish populations, but only 7 (9.6%) were inhabited by trout (either brook char, rainbow or brown trout). Tui chub (*Siphateles bicolor*) was the most widespread of 9 fish species, occurring in 5 lakes. Of the salmonids, rainbow trout occurred in 4 lakes, and brook char and brown trout each occurred in 2 lakes. Other species included redside shiner (2 lakes), Tahoe sucker (2 lakes), golden shiner (2 lakes), speckled dace (3 lakes) and fathead minnow (1 lake). Fish-bearing lakes were on average larger, deeper, and occurred at lower elevations than fishless lakes and included 6 of the 10 largest lakes in the park. Chlorophyll-a concentrations were 6-fold higher and light transparency (Secchi depth) approximately 50% lower in fish-bearing lakes. Fish-bearing lakes also had higher average pH and specific conductance, and experienced greater hypolimnetic oxygen depletion, than fishless lakes illustrating large differences in overall productivity. Strong, trophically mediated fish effects were observed among littoral macroinvertebrates with many large, mobile taxa (Trichoptera, Odonata, Dytiscidae, Notonectidae and Corixidae) having significantly lower densities in fish-bearing lakes, across 3 different habitats (vegetated, soft sediments, and coarse sediments). Reduction in large invertebrate predators in soft and coarse sediment habitats resulted in an indirect positive effect on small-bodied Chironomidae larvae. Differences in zooplankton distribution were less obvious, due in large part to seasonal variation in zooplankton abundance and phenology and differences among sampling dates, which extended over several weeks. In general, both crustacean zooplankton and rotifers had higher densities in fish-bearing lakes, probably due to greater overall productivity in larger, mesotrophic lakes. Fish effects were observed among three of the largest zooplankton species, however, with a large diaptomid copepod (*Hesperodiaptomus kenai*), phantom midge larva (*Chaoborus americanus*) and fairy shrimp (*Steptocephalus sealii*) only occurring in fishless lakes. The policy of discontinuing stocking of non-native fishes in National Parks has been largely successful in many (approx. 90%) natural lakes in LVNP to return to their historic fishless condition. Only the largest, most productive lakes and smaller lakes with suitable spawning habitat continue to support fish populations. Strong trophically mediated fish effects are likely to persist within these few lakes.

Acknowledgements

This study was supported financially through cooperative agreement CA9320A004 with the Klamath Network Inventory and Monitoring Program of the U.S. National Park Service, and was a collaborative project including Southern Oregon University, National Park Service and Redwood Sciences Laboratory of the U.S. Forest Service. Jon Stead (RSL) was crew leader, and did a masterful job with logistics and coordinating field surveys. Miranda Haggarty (RSL) contributed greatly to all field-sampling efforts. Southern Oregon University biology and environmental studies students Jessie Goldstein, Lyndia Hammer, Kate Meyer, and Jon Speece were responsible for collecting littoral macroinvertebrate and zooplankton samples, and contributed to fish and amphibian surveys. They, along with Erim Gomez, John Prunty, and Aaron Maxwell sorted samples in the laboratory and assisted with laboratory analyses. Considerable logistic support was provided by Don Ashton and Hartwell Welsh (Redwood Sciences Lab), Nancy Nordensten and Michael Magnuson (Lassen Volcanic National Park) and Daniel Sarr, Bob Truitt and Matt Cofer (Klamath Network I & M Program). This study was conducted under Scientific Research and Collecting Permit number LAVO-2004-SCI-0015, issued to M. S. Parker.

Introduction

Stocking of nonnative fishes into historically fishless lakes represents one of the most widespread manipulations of high elevation aquatic ecosystems throughout mountainous regions of western North America (Bahls 1992, Knapp et al. 2001a, Dunham et al. 2004, Pister 2001). Ecological impacts of nonnative fish introductions have been well documented and include dramatic reductions and extirpations of large, mobile benthic invertebrate and zooplankton species (Bradford et al. 1998, Carlisle & Hawkins 1998, Parker et al. 2001, Stoddard 1987; but see Wissinger et al. 2006 for contrasting results from New Zealand lakes) and amphibian populations (Bradford 1989, Bull & Marx 2002, Knapp 2005, Pilliod & Peterson 2001). Major alterations of lake communities in response to fish introductions or changes in fish abundance can lead to large-scale changes in ecological processes (Walters & Vincent 1973, Elser et al. 1995, Carpenter and Kitchell 1993, Schindler et al. 2001) and may extend into the terrestrial environment (Matthews, et al. 2002).

Cessation of fish stocking in the 1970s and 80s within national parks and some wilderness areas has resulted in many smaller lakes returning to a fishless condition, but self-sustaining fish populations continue to persist in most larger lakes (Donald 1987, Knapp 1996, Armstrong and Knapp 2004). Lack of systematic surveys in many areas, however, limits our knowledge of current fish distributions and ongoing impacts on native biota (Bahls 1992). In this study we determined (1) the distribution of introduced fishes among larger, natural lakes within Lassen Volcanic National Park (LVNP), (2) ongoing fish effects on littoral macroinvertebrate and zooplankton assemblages, and (3) the extent to which these assemblages have responded to the cessation of fish stocking and return of some lakes to a fishless condition. Because it is likely that most, if not all, natural lakes >2 m deep within LVNP were stocked at some time in the past, currently fishless lakes would have lost their fish populations since the cessation of stocking in the late 1970s. Differences in invertebrate distribution and abundance between fish-bearing and fishless lakes should, therefore, reveal changes in response to fish loss and show whether communities within previously stocked lakes are resilient to major shifts in top predator abundance.

This was a companion study to the survey of fish and amphibian distributions reported by Stead et al. (2005), which was the first comprehensive survey of lakes within LVNP. Their survey, which included surveys of wilderness areas adjacent to LVNP, showed that certain palatable amphibian species and fairy shrimp were significantly less likely to inhabit lentic habitats with fish.

Methods

Fish Surveys
Whereas the goal of the companion study (Stead et al. 2005) was to visit and survey every lentic habitat within the park boundaries, including lakes, ponds, and wetlands, this study focused on larger lakes and ponds that are currently inhabited by fish, were previously stocked, or that could potentially have been stocked or colonized by fish in the past. Survey crews visited 365 different lentic water bodies during summer 2004, including 57 lakes (>0.5 hectare surface area), 94 permanent ponds (<0.5 hectare surface area), 174 temporary ponds, and 40 wet meadows (see Stead et al. 2005 for detailed descriptions of survey methods and habitat characteristics measured). A combination of visual surveys and gillnet sets were used to determine fish presence and abundance among larger permanent ponds and lakes. Gill net sets were typically 4hr (range 4-7 hr), but at 14 pond sites sets were shorter (approximately 2-3.5 hr) because the entire bottom and water column were visible and visual surveys confirmed the absence of fish. Gill nets were made of sinking monofilament, 36 m long by 1.8 m tall comprised of six 6 m long panels with mess sizes ranging from 10 – 38 mm, and effectively captured fish ranging from small trout and cyprinids (> 60 mm FL) to large trout (up to 460 mm FL). All fish captured in gill nets were identified to species, weighed to the nearest 1.0 g using a spring-loaded balance, and measured (TL and FL to the nearest mm).

Littoral Macroinvertebrates
We used D-framed dip nets (0.5 mm mesh) to collect samples of littoral macroinvertbrates by making a number of "standard sweeps" along the lake bottom 1-2 m from shore. A standard sweep consisted of two 1 m passes of the D-net approximately parallel to the shoreline and following the contour of the lake bottom. An initial pass in one direction was immediately followed by a return pass over the same area in the opposite direction. We collected samples from three broadly-defined habitats, (1) vegetated areas with submerged and/or emergent vegetation, (2) exposed soft bottom habitats of either fine organic or inorganic sediments, and (3) bare, rocky substrates, with 3-6 sweeps taken from each habitat. Samples were approximately equally spaced throughout a given habitat within a lake, though in many lakes one or more of these littoral habitats did not occur (Table 1). This sampling method effectively collects benthic organisms residing on and within the upper layers of the substratum and nektonic organisms in the water column above the substratum. Samples were preserved (80% ethyl alcohol) and returned to the laboratory where all macroinvertebrates were sorted from organic and inorganic debris under 10X magnification with a dissecting microscope. Organisms were identified to the lowest practical taxonomic level (genus or species for most insects, family for the Chironomidae) and enumerated. Density estimates are reported as number of individuals per standard sweep.

Zooplankton
Zooplankton samples were collected by making vertical tows through the water column with a standard 13 cm diameter 63 μm mesh Wisconsin-style plankton net. Sampling was done from a float tube near the deepest portion of each lake. The net was lowered to within 0.5 m of the lake bottom and slowly retrieved to the surface. From 3-5 tows were made from selected lakes (Table 1). Individual tows were combined into a single composite sample for each lake, fixed in the field using sugar formalin solution (4% final concentration; Haney and Hall 1973) and returned to the laboratory for analysis. Total volume of lake water sampled was estimated as the product

3

of tow depth, area of the net opening (0.013 m^2), and number of tows. Zooplankton densities were uncorrected for net efficiency and likely underestimate actual densities, but should not affect relative density differences among lakes.

In the laboratory, concentrated plankton samples were brought to a standard volume (50 or 100 ml depending on zooplankton density) thoroughly mixed using a vortex mixer or by aspiration, subsampled, and enumerated. A minimum of 5 1 ml subsamples was enumerated for each sample. Subsamples were drawn using a wide-mouth volumetric pipette, placed in a gridded Sedgewick-Rafter counting cell, and observed at 10 -40 X magnification under a dissecting microscope. Zooplankton were identified to the lowest practical taxonomic level (usually genus). Rotifers were identified at higher magnification (100-400 X) using a compound light microscope.

Limnological Characteristics

From 15-21 August we measured limnological characteristics of a subset of fish-bearing (N = 9) and fishless (N = 13) lakes. We selected this restricted time period late in the summer to minimize variation in productivity and water quality among lakes due to seasonal differences and because ongoing surveys revealed which lakes were inhabited by fish. The subset of fishless lakes was selected to represent (1) the range of surface areas and depths across all lakes > 2m deep, (2) lakes known to have been stocked in the past and thus to have lost their fish populations, and (3) lakes distributed across the park to incorporate differences in geographic setting among hydrologic units (based on the California Interagency Watershed Map of 1999). One fish-bearing lake (Cal Waters site 10956 in Blue Lake Canyon) was not sampled because of its remote location and difficult access.

Secchi depth was measured to the nearest 0.1 m from a small boat or float tube near the deepest portion of each lake. At two lakes, one fishless (Drake Lake) and one inhabited by brook char (Ridge Lake), the lake bottom was visible from the surface in the deepest area, so Secchi depth was not measured.

To estimate phytoplankton biomass, integrated water samples (approximately 1.5 L) were collected from the upper 2.5 m of the water column of each lake using a 3 m long by 2.54 cm diameter flexible tube. 0.5-2 L of lake water was filtered through a Gelman A/E glass fiber filter and the filters were placed in aluminum foil covered Petri dishes, stored on dry ice, and returned to the laboratory for pigment analysis. In the laboratory, photosynthetic pigments were extracted in 90% buffered acetone solution (24 hr at 4 °C in the dark) and concentrations measured spectrophotometrically using the monochromatic method (Lorenzen 1967). Algal cells were disrupted to facilitate the extraction process by placing filters in glass centrifuge tubes and grinding them for approximately 1 minute with a nylon tissue grinder in a small volume of buffered acetone solution. Following the extraction period, samples were centrifuged (3,000 rpm) for 3-5 minutes and approximately 5 ml of supernatant was placed in spectrophotometer cuvette for analysis. Phytoplankton biomass is reported as μg/L chlorophyll-a.

At each lake standard water quality parameters (including pH, specific conductance, dissolved oxygen, and temperature) were measured using a calibrated YSI 556 multiprobe instrument. In addition, at 6 fish-bearing and 3 fishless lakes vertical profiles of temperature and dissolved oxygen were measured to determine if deeper lakes become thermally stratified and experience hypolimnetic oxygen depletion.

Table 1. Benthic macroinvertebrate and zooplankton sampling effort distributed among lakes with and without fish. Benthic samples are number of D-net sweeps within a given broadly-defined habitat type. If there is no value listed for a habitat, that habitat was not present within the lake. Zooplankton samples are number of vertical tows with a Wisconsin-style plankton net.

| | Benthic Sample | | | Zooplankton |
	Vegetation	Fine Sediments	Coarse Sediments	
Fish Lakes				
Summit	3	3		6
Ridge		5	5	3
Blue Lake Canyon		4		4
Butte	6	6		5
Snag	3	3	6	5
Horseshoe	3	5		5
Manzanita	5	5		5
Juniper	5	5	5	5
Reflection	4	4	4	4
Widow	3	5	5	3
Fishless Lakes				
Bathtub (N)	3	4		
Bathtub (S)	5	5		5
Big Bear		3	3	
Bluff		5		
Cluster #1		4		
Cluster #2	5			
Cluster #5	3	3		5
Crumbaugh	3	3	4	
Crystal	3	4	5	
Drake	5	5	5	5
East	3	3	3	
Echo	3	5	4	
Emerald		3	5	3
Emigrant	4	3		
Feather		5	3	
Glenn	5	5		5
Helen			5	
Hidden	4	3		4
Indian	5			3
Island	5			
Jakey	3	3	3	3
Little Bear	4	3		
Lower Twin	5		5	5
No Name (#10422)	3			
Rainbow	5	4		
Shadow		4		

Table 1 (Continued). Benthic macroinvertebrate and zooplankton sampling effort distributed among lakes with and without fish. Benthic samples are number of D-net sweeps within a given broadly-defined habitat type. If there is no value listed for a habitat, that habitat was not present within the lake. Zooplankton samples are number of vertical tows with a Wisconsin-style plankton net.

| | Benthic Sample | | | Zooplankton |
	Vegetation	Fine Sediments	Coarse Sediments	
Sifford #1	3	3	4	
Sifford #5	3	3	3	
Sifford #9		3	4	
Silver		4	4	
Soap	4			
Soda	3	3		
Swan	3	3		5
Terrace	3	3		5
Upper Twin	5	5		

Results

Fish Distribution

Among the 151 lakes and permanent ponds surveyed, 73 were natural water bodies greater than 2 m deep and included most of the lakes known to have been stocked with trout in the past. Among these, only 10 (13.7%) were inhabited by fish with a total of 9 species captured or observed (Table 2). Only 7 lakes (9.6%) were inhabited by salmonids. Three lakes were inhabited by a single salmonid species (either brook char or rainbow trout), 3 by one or more cyprinid species (dominated by tui chub, Lahontan redside, or golden shiners), and 4 lakes had mixed assemblages of trout and cyprinids or trout, cyprinids and a catostomid. Summit and Ridge lakes were inhabited by brook char and were the only two lakes inhabited by the same fish species. The remaining 8 lakes each had a unique combination of species (Table 2).

Table 2. Fish species and catch per unit effort (no/gill net hr) among LNVP lakes, summer 2004.

	Rainbow trout	Brook char	Brown trout	Tui chub	Speckled dace	Lahontan shiner	Golden shiner	Fathead minnow	Tahoe sucker
Blue Lake Canyon	8.75								
Ridge		1.25							
Summit		3.00							
Butte	0.44			6.59	0.00[a]	9.01			14.73
Horseshoe		1.19		4.16					
Manzanita	0.83	1.22			0.00[a]		0.00[b]		
Snag	1.70			0.24					0.73
Juniper				0.00[c]		1.33			
Reflection							63.83	0.22	
Widow				6.23	0.00[a]				

[a]speckled dace observed within and near inlet and outlet streams, but not captured in gill nets.
[b]observed in the lake, but not captured in gill net
[c]found dead along shoreline, but not captured in gill net

Fish were unequally distributed among lakes based on lake size. Average surface area and depth were significantly greater for fish-bearing versus fishless lakes (p=0.0012 and p=0.0149 for surface area and depth comparisons respectively; Mann-Whitney U), and the range of lake sizes and depths was also much greater, in spite of there being many fewer fish-bearing lakes (Fig. 1). Fish-bearing lakes included the 4 largest lakes in the park (Juniper, Snag, Butte, and Horseshoe) and 6 of the largest 10. Average elevation of fishless lakes (mean ± 1SE = 2,104 m ± 19.35) was significantly greater (p = 0.037 ; Mann-Whitney U) than for fish-bearing lakes (1,998 m ± 63.69), and fishless lakes occurred across a broader range of elevations (Fig. 1).

Catch rates (CPUE = fish/gillnet hr) varied considerably among lakes. CPUE for salmonid species appeared to be somewhat higher in lakes in which they occurred alone than lakes in which they occurred with cyprinid and/or catostomid species. However, small sample sizes and large variation in lake size, and thus sampling effort differences among lakes, limit meaningful comparisons of fish densities as estimated by CPUE.

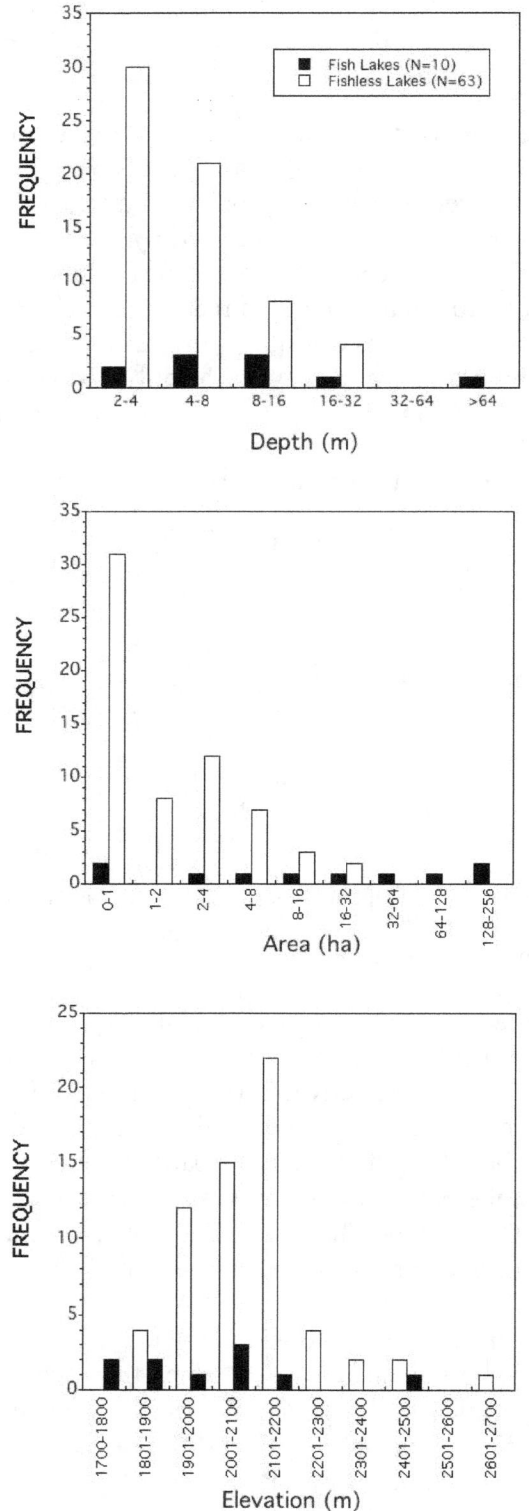

Figure 1. Frequency distributions of depth, surface area, and eleveation for fish-bearing and fishless lakes.

Littoral Macroinvertebrates

Macroinvertebrate distribution and abundance differed considerably between fish-bearing and fishless lakes, and among lakes with different fish species compositions (Table 3). Across the 3 broad habitats sampled, macroinvertebrate density was generally greatest within aquatic vegetation and lowest within coarse sediments (Figure 2). Although there was considerable variation in macroinvertebrate abundance and diversity among lakes, and large disparities in sample sizes between fish and fishless lakes, there were clear density differences, particularly for large, mobile taxa (Figure 2). For example, within both vegetated and fine sediment habitats, caddisfly larvae (Trichoptera), damselfly and dragonfly nymphs (Zygoptera and Anisoptera respectively), and waterboatmen and backswimmers (Corixidae and Notonectidae respectively) had higher densities in the absence of fish. In coarse sediment habitats predaceous diving beetle larvae (Dytiscidae), along with the Trichoptera, Odonata (both Zygoptera and Anisoptera), and Corixidae, were more abundant in fishless lakes. In contrast to these large, mobile taxa, larval Chironomidae had significantly higher densities in fine and coarse sediment habitats in fish-bearing lakes (Figure 3), but there was no significant difference in their densities between fish-bearing and fishless lakes in vegetated habitats.

Table 3. Summary of benthic and nektonic macroinvertebrate taxa collected among lakes with different fish assemblages.

	Salmonids (N=3)	Cyprinids (N=3)	Mixed spp. (N=4)	Fishless (N=32)
Ephemeroptera				
Caenis sp.	X	X	X	X
Callibaetis spp.	X	X	X	X
Odonata				
Zygoptera				
Coenagrion/Enallagma spp.	X		X	X
Lestes sp.	X	X		X
Zoniagrion excalamationis	X	X		
Anisoptera				
Aeshna spp.	X	X	X	X
Cordulia shurtleffi	X			X
Pachydiplax longipennis		X		X
Sympetrum spp.				X
Hemiptera				
Belostoma sp.				X
Corisella decolor	X	X	X	X
Notonecta undulata	X	X	X	X
Ranatra brevicola				X
Gerris remigis	X	X		X
Microvelia sp.				X
Megaloptera				
Sialis sp.	X	X	X	X
Trichoptera				
Desmona sp.	X			X
Gumaga sp.			X	
Limnephilus spp.	X	X	X	X
Oecetis disjunctus		X	X	X

Table 3 (Continued). Summary of benthic and nektonic macroinvertebrate taxa collected among lakes with different fish assemblages.

Coleoptera				
Dytiscidae				
Agabus spp.	X	X		X
Copelatus sp.				
Coptotomus longulus	X			X
Dytiscus spp.	X			
Graphoderus	X			X
Hydroporus sp.			X	X
Hygrotus spp.				X
Rhantus sp.				X
Sanfillipodytes spp.				X
Thermonectus sp.				X
Gyrinidae				
Gyrinus sp.				X
Hydrophilidae				
Tropisternus sp.				X
Diptera				
Chironomidae	X	X	X	X
Ceratopogonidae			X	X
Culicidae				X
Non-Insecta				
Crustacea				
Branchiopoda				
Streptocephalis sealii				X
Holopedium gibberum				X
Amphipoda				
Hyalella azteca		X	X	X
Decapoda				
Pacifistacus leniusculus			X	
Annelida				
Oligochaeta	X	X	X	X
Hirundinea				X
Mollusca				
Sphaeriidae		X	X	
Planorbidae				X
Acari	X	X	X	X
Total	20	18	18	39

10

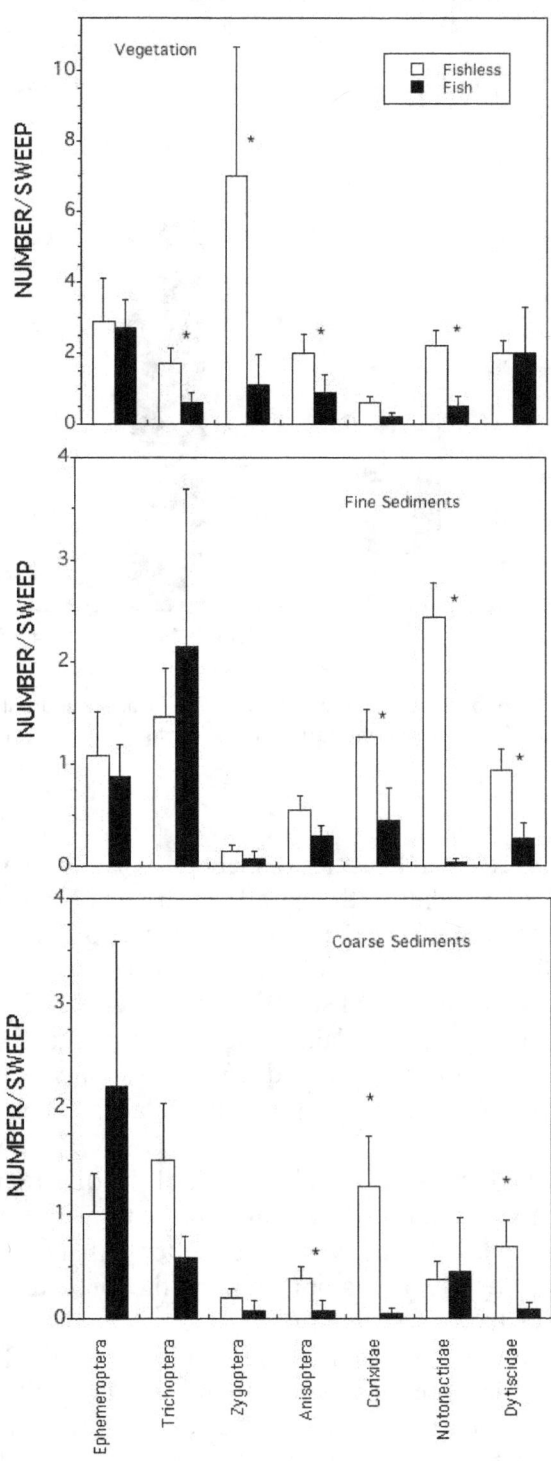

Figure 2 Comparison of littoral macroinvertebrate densities in vegetated, soft-sediment, and coarse sediment habitats between fish-bearing and fishless lakes. Asterisks indicate statistically significant difference (Mann-Whitney U; p<0.05)

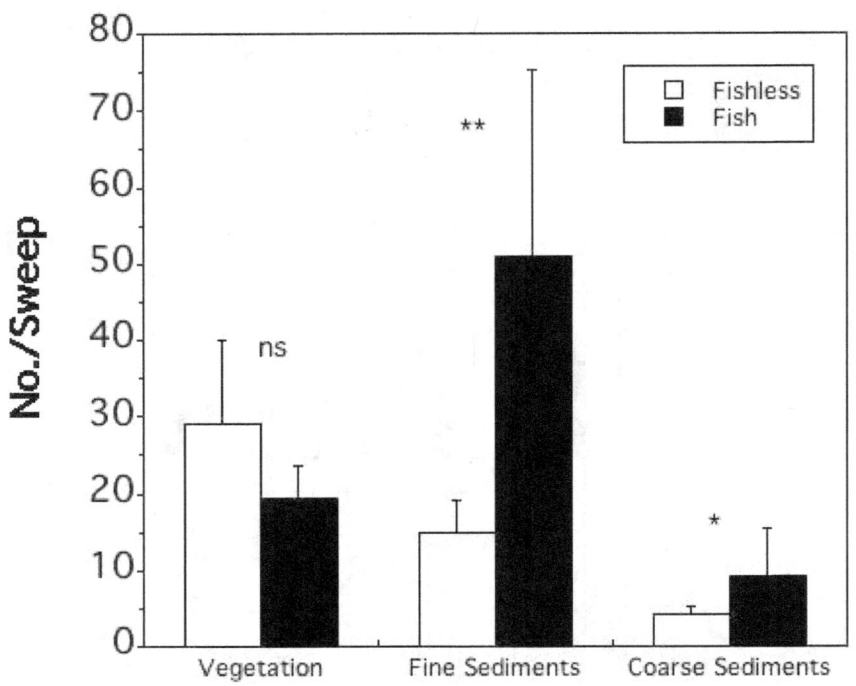

Figure 3. Comparison of larval Chironomidae densities between fish-bearing and fishless lakes, and among habitats. Values are means ± 1 S.E. and asterisks indicate that differences are significantly different (Mann-Whitney U, p<0.05).

Zooplankton

Zooplankton abundance (Figure 4) and species distribution (Table 4) also differed significantly between fish-bearing and fishless lakes with overall densities of both crustaceans and rotifers being much greater in fish-bearing lakes (Figure 4). Densities of *Bosmina longirostris* were significantly higher (p = 0.021; Kruskall-Wallis test) in cyprinid-bearing lakes (either cyprinids alone or in mixed species assemblages) and small cyclopoid copepods were significantly more abundant (p = 0.043) in mixed fish species lakes. Both taxa are more susceptible to invertebrate predators than fish. *Hesperodiaptomus kenai* and *Chaoborus americanus*, both predators of small crustacean zooplankton, were only found in fishless lakes (Table 4).

Because of the small number of lakes inhabited by each of the different fish assemblages, and extreme differences among them and thus large variation in total and species-specific zooplankton densities, there appear to be few general patterns that can be attributed to the distribution and abundance of fish. For example, among the three lakes inhabited by single trout species (Ridge, Summit and Blue Lake Canyon) *Daphnia rosea* densities ranged from 0 (Ridge Lakes) to 37/L (Blue Lake Canyon), *Diaptomus* spp. ranged from 0 (Blue Lake Canyon) to 62.5/L (Ridge Lakes), cyclopoid copepods were only present in 1 of the 3 lakes (Blue Lake Canyon), and total rotifer abundance varied nearly 30-fold among them. Similar differences were observed among lakes with cyprinids only and lakes with mixed fish species assemblages. These large disparities among lakes are likely due to seasonal differences in zooplankton communities that were sampled across several weeks of the summer.

Table 4. Zooplankton taxa collected among lakes with different fish assemblages.

	Salmonids (N=3)	Cyprinids (N=3)	Mixed spp. (N=4)	Fishless (N=32)
Rotifera				
Brachionus	X	X	X	X
Gastropus			X	X
Lecane	X	X	X	
Keratella	X		X	X
Polyarthra	X	X	X	X
Asplanchna	X	X	X	
Kellicottia longispina	X	X	X	X
Synchaeta	X		X	
Cladocera				
Bosmina longirostris	X	X	X	X
Chydorus sphaericus		X		X
Daphnia rosea	X	X	X	X
Copepoda				
Hesperodiaptomus kenai				X
Diaptomus spp.	X	X	X	X
Cyclopoida spp.	X	X	X	X
Anostraca				
Streptocephalus sealii				X
Insecta				
Chaoborus americanus				X

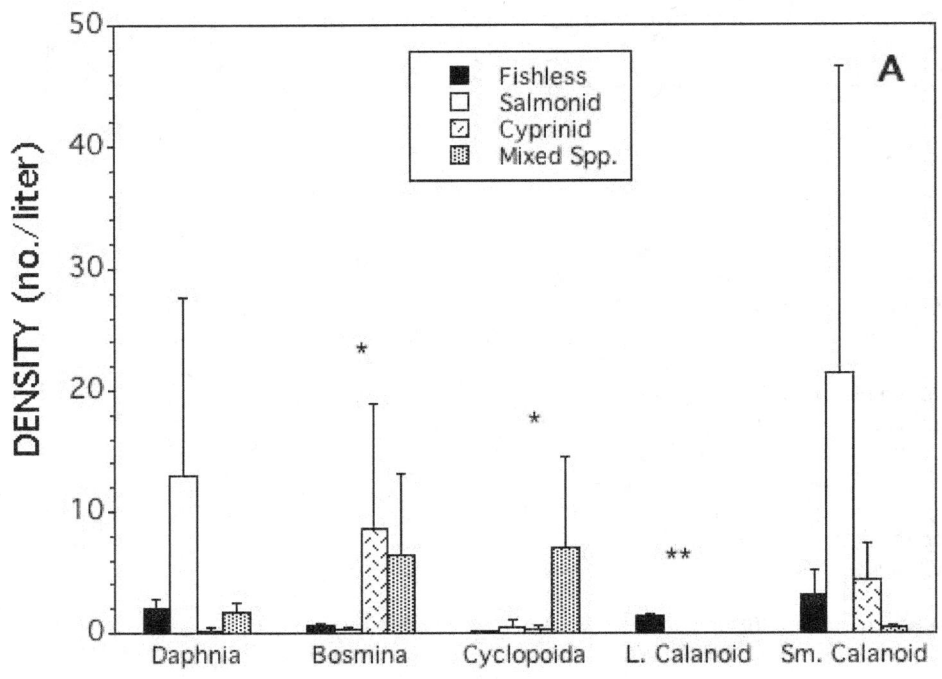

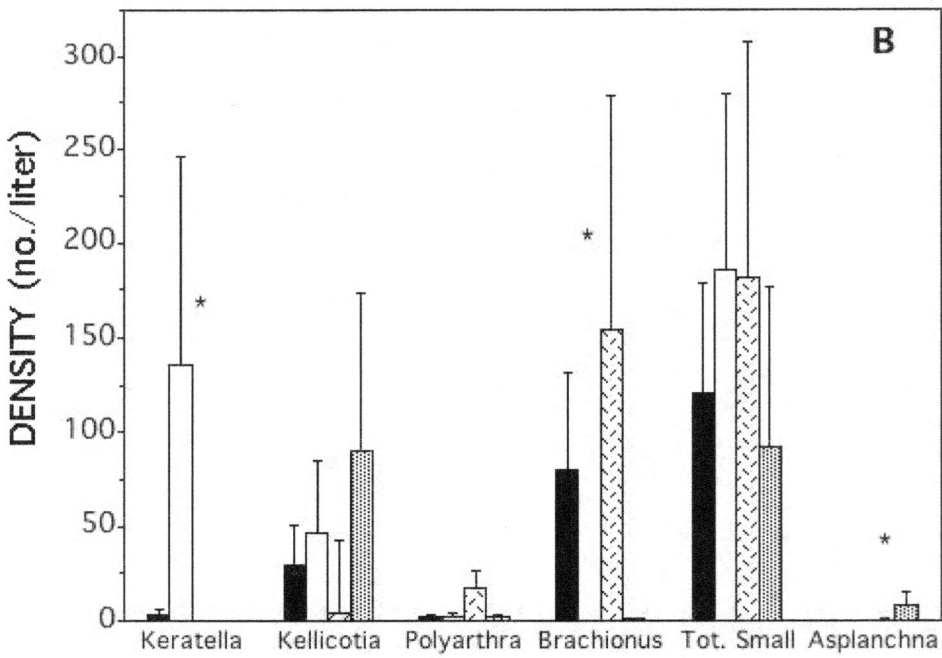

Figure 4. Comparisons of (A) crustacean zooplankton and (B) rotifer densities among fish-bearing and fishless lakes (values are means and error bars are ± 1 SE). Asterisks indicate statistically significant differences (Kruskall-Wallis; * p<0.05, ** p<0.01).

Limnological Characteristics

Fish-bearing lakes had significantly higher average chlorophyll concentrations (p=0.0008; Mann-Whitney U) and shallower Secchi depths (p=0.0077) than fishless lakes (Table 5). In addition, pH was slightly, but significantly, higher (p=0.023; Mann-Whitney) and conductivity was higher, but not significantly (p=0.057), in fish-bearing versus fishless lakes (Table 5). Vertical profiles of temperature and dissolved oxygen (Figure 5) show that all 9 lakes for which data were collected experience some degree of thermal stratification during the summer. Of the 6 fish lakes measured, 4 (Butte, Snag, Widow and Summit) showed substantial hypolimnetic oxygen depletion characteristic of productive, mesotrophic to eutrophic lakes (Wetzel 2001). The 3 fishless lakes for which we were able to collect vertical profile data had lower average surface temperatures (19.13±1.12 °C vs. 21.17±0.13 °C; mean ± 1SE), somewhat deeper and and less distinct thermoclines, and less pronounced hypolimnetic oxygen depletion than most of the fish-bearing lakes. Juniper Lake, the largest, deepest lake in LVNP is clearly oligotrophic compared to the other fish-bearing lakes as shown by its relatively high light transparency, low chlorophyll-a concentration (Table 5) and orthograde oxygen curve (Figure 5). Water quality parameter values reported here reflect conditions similar to those reported over several years from the 1960s-90s (National Park Service Water Resources Division 1999).

Table 5. Comparisons of water quality parameters between fish and fishless lakes.

	Chl. A (mg/L)	Secchi Depth (m)	pH	Specific Conductance (μS/cm)	Date
Fishless Lakes					
Bathtub (S)	0.52	5.9	7.2	46.9	15 Aug
Drake	1.16	--	7.3	36.5	18 Aug
Emerald	0.20	7.0	6.8	11.2	19 Aug
Glenn	1.22	5.3	6.9	25.8	17 Aug
Hidden	0.61	5.4	6.4	28.6	16 Aug
Indian	3.10	4.3	7.1	32.2	17 Aug
Jakey	0.44	6.6	7.1	30.0	17 Aug
Lower Twin	0.91	6.5	6.8	24.0	16 Aug
Rainbow	0.66	6.6	6.7	18.1	16 Aug
Shadow	0.10	21.5	7.1	10.0	18 Aug
S. Cluster	2.88	3.6	7.6	41.5	19 Aug
Swan	0.33	6.3	6.5	26.2	16 Aug
Terrace	0.24	8.3	7.0	12.0	18 Aug
Mean (± 1 SE)	0.95 ± 0.27	7.28 ± 1.34	7.0 ± 0.1	26.4 ± 3.2	
Fish Lakes					
Summit	4.21	4.5	7.1	13.3	19 Aug
Ridge	1.12	--	7.0	8.4	18 Aug
Butte	4.85	4.2	7.4	55.0	15 Aug
Manzanita	4.80	4.2	8.1	85.2	21 Aug
Snag	7.20	2.3	7.2	51.0	15 Aug
Horseshoe	18.12	2.4	7.7	46.9	17 Aug
Juniper	1.08	6.8	6.8	28.0	17 Aug
Reflection	7.20	2.5	8.2	80.0	21 Aug
Widow	8.10	2.0	7.6	48.2	15 Aug
Mean (± 1 SE)	6.29 ± 1.70	3.61 ± 0.58	7.5 ± 0.2	46.2 ± 8.8	

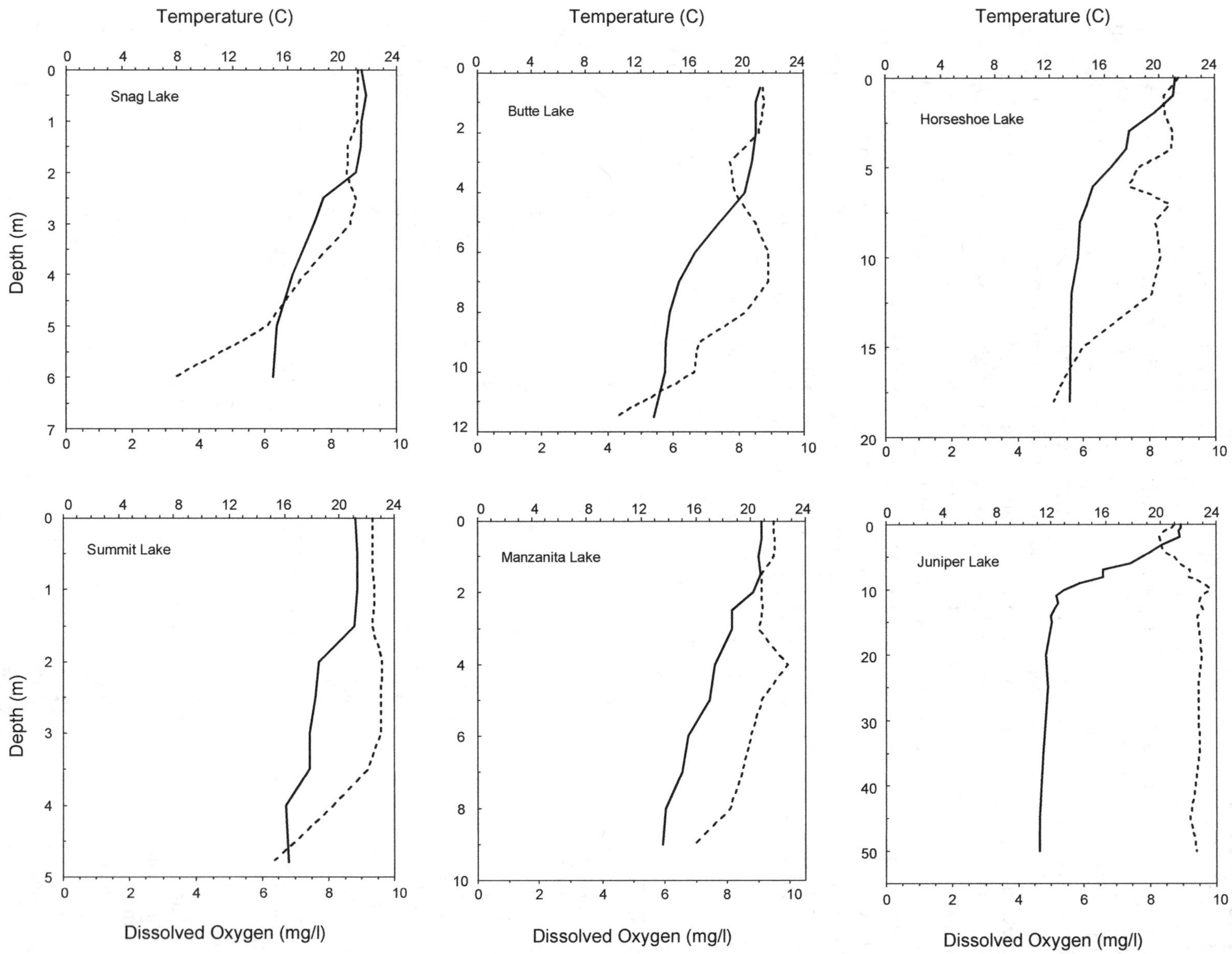

Figure 5. Vertical profiles of temperature and dissolved oxygen for 6 fish-bearing and 3 fishless lakes, 15-21 August 2004.

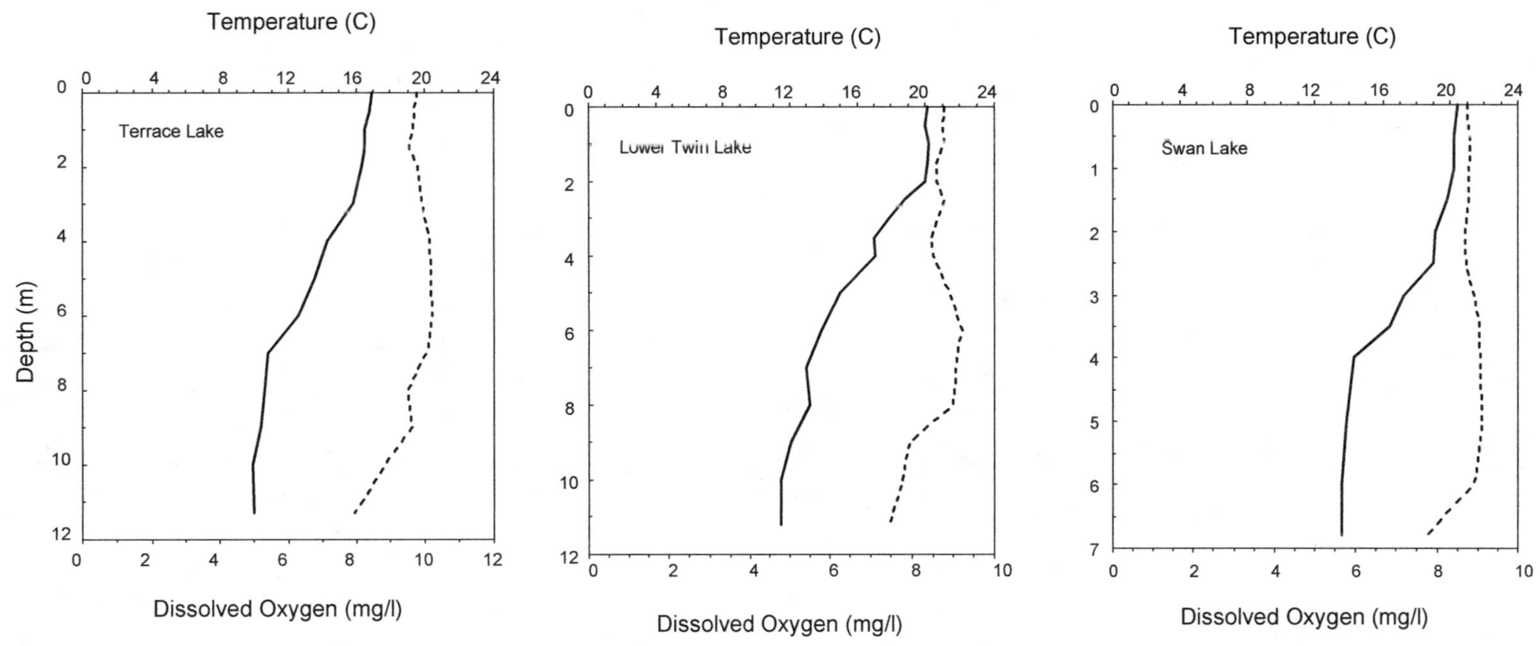

Figure 5 (continued). Vertical profiles of temperature and dissolved oxygen for 6 fish-bearing and 3 fishless lakes, 15-21 August 2004.

Discussion

Fish stocking in what is now LVNP began as early as the late 1800s with the arrival of Euro-American settlers and became more extensive during the early to mid 1900s as the California Department of Fish and Game (CDFG) gained control of stocking programs statewide (Wallis 1977). Stocking records (e.g., as summarized by Dennison 1977) and anecdotal reports (e.g., Drost 1991) show that at least 42 lakes were stocked during the 1960s and 70s. Of these, 37 were stocked regularly (at least every 2 yr), while others were stocked less frequently (in some cases only once). Unfortunately, the records are not complete and it is likely that fish were introduced more widely, particularly during early years of fish stocking. Movement of fish among lakes by anglers was probably also common as shown by the current distribution of non-game "bait" species and past reports and current distributions of fish in lakes not included in stocking records. For example, records show that only brook char and rainbow trout were historically stocked into Horseshoe Lake, but our surveys captured only brown trout and tui chub. Tui chub, Lahontan redside, speckled dace, and Tahoe sucker are native to, and likely bait bucket introductions from, the Eagle Lake or Susan River systems east of LVNP (Moyle 2002). Combinations of these species are found within large lakes on the east side of the park, and are known to have been introduced by anglers in lakes and reservoirs outside of, but within watersheds draining the park (Moyle 2002). Though not indicated in stocking records, golden shiners were probably introduced by CDFG into Manzanita Lake as forage for introduced brown and rainbow trout (Dill and Cordone 1997), and subsequently colonized and became the dominant fish species in Reflection Lake. Thus, unrecorded, intentional stocking of nonnative fishes and anglers moving fish among lakes probably resulted in a wider distribution than records indicate and it is likely that most, if not all, larger ponds and lakes had fish introduced into them at some time in the past. With the cessation of fish stocking in the late 1970s, and prior to that for lakes stocked less frequently, many lakes have reverted back to a fishless condition.

Perhaps the most striking result of this study was the limited distribution of fish among natural lakes within LVNP (13.7% including all species, but only 9.6 % with trout). Stead et al. (2005) reported that of 365 sites visited, 23 (6.3%) were inhabited by fish. Of those, 9 were reported to be lakes, 4 were permanent and 2 temporary ponds, and 8 were wet meadows. The temporary pond and wet meadow sites were associated with perennial, fish-bearing streams. Of the fish-bearing permanent pond sites, two were small, artificial impoundments and a third was a very small (<0.09 hectare surface area) rock pool located in the Fantastic Lava Beds (Cal Waters site 10412), within 200 m of and with a subsurface hydrologic connection to Butte Lake. This site was inhabited by a large population of small cyprinids, either tui chub or speckled dace, which are also present in Butte Lake. Hat Lake is a flooded meadow within the West Fork Hat Creek stream channel created by the Highway 89 road crossing and enhanced by beavers. Dream Lake is created by earthen berms built to impound the flows of several springbrook tributaries of Hot Springs Creek in the Drakesbad area of Warner Valley. Both impoundments were historically stocked (rainbow trout and brook char in Dream and Hat lakes respectively) and continue to support trout populations as artificial lentic habitats within fish-bearing streams. Because these 3 sites were not representative of natural lakes with the park, they were not included in this analysis.

The nearly 90% of historically-stocked lakes in LVNP that are now fishless is much higher compared to most mountainous regions of western North America. For example, Bahls (1992) predicted that approximately 60% of all originally fishless lakes, and 95% of larger (>2 ha), deeper (>3m) lakes, are inhabited by introduced trout populations. Armstrong and Knapp (2004) estimated that over 60% of the originally-stocked lakes in the central and southern Sierra Nevada continued to support self-sustaining trout populations 4-8 years after the cessation of stocking. Stead et al. (2005) reported that 42-73% of lakes in two wilderness areas adjacent to LVNP were inhabited by trout. Among factors likely contributing to such disparities is the small proportion of fishless LVNP lakes that have perennial inlets and outlets (<10%) and therefore lack suitable spawning habitat. The majority of fish-bearing lakes have perennial inlets and outlets that provide spawning habitat and are linked to major stream drainages with self-sustaining fish populations. There is a distinct precipitation gradient across the park (Clow et al. 2003), with the more mountainous western side receiving a greater snow pack and more overall precipitation than the drier eastern side. The density of lake basins is greater on the eastern side of the park, however, which may affect the supply of surface runoff to many lakes, particularly during typically dry summers. Porous volcanic soils and bedrock may also permit precipitation and snowmelt to rapidly penetrate the groundwater, supplying springs throughout the park but possibly limiting surface flows into and out of most lakes, thereby restricting both connectivity among water bodies and spawning habitat within them. The lack of suitable spawning habitat and the potential for winterkill are likely responsible for the loss of fish populations in most lakes. Large differences in chlorophyll concentrations, Secchi depth, and pH show that, in general, the lakes that continue to support fish populations include the largest, most productive lakes in the park.

In addition to having a much lower proportion of fish-bearing natural lakes than most mountainous regions of western North America, species composition among LVNP lakes is also much different. Rainbow trout and brook char have been the most widely introduced fishes into mountain lakes and are currently the most widespread species with self-sustaining populations (Donald 1987, Bahls 1992, Dill and Cardone 1997, Drake and Naiman 2000, Dunham et al. 2004). Non-salmonid species are typically rare in mountain lakes (e.g., Armstrong and Knapp 2004). Our survey results show that tui chub is the most widely distributed species, occurring in 5 lakes (50%), and cyprinds, overall, were found in 70% of fish-bearing lakes, the same proportion as salmonid species. Thus, fish species likely introduced through bait bucket releases by anglers are as widespread as salmonid species intentionally introduced to establish recreational fisheries. Three lakes, Manzanita, Butte, and Blue Lake Canyon (site 10956), are the only natural lakes likely to have been inhabited by fish historically. Unlike the lakes within the park, all major streams (Kings, Hot Springs, Hat, Grassy Swale, Manzanita, Butte, Lost, and N.F. Bailey creeks, and tributaries to Mill Cr.) are inhabited by introduced trout.

The lack of fish distribution surveys in the past precludes being able to determine when specific lakes became fishless, making it impossible to track temporal patterns in responses of aquatic communities to changes in the intensity of fish predation. Numerous studies have shown that introduced fishes drastically alter lake food webs by reducing abundances of or eliminating large invertebrate species (e.g., Brooks and Dodson 1965, Northcote et al. 1978, Luecke 1990, Chess et al. 1993). Results of this study show a similar pattern, with many large, mobile macroinvertebrate taxa having reduced densities across habitats in fish-bearing versus fishless lakes. Indirect positive effects of fish predation on Chironomidae densities within fine and coarse sediments (but not more complex vegetated habitats) show that trophically-mediated fish effects are strong within these habitats. Higher densities of larger mobile taxa among habitats in lakes that were historically stocked but are now fishless suggest that these populations are relatively resilient to major shifts in fish distribution, at least within the 20-30 year timeframe since fish were last stocked. Knapp et al (2001b) showed similar responses of littoral benthos in Sierra Nevada lakes that returned to being fishless after having been stocked for several years.

Zooplankton assemblages showed much less obvious differences between fish-bearing and fishless lakes with the exception of three large, conspicuous taxa. The large calanoid copepod *Hesperodiaptomus kenai* was found in 8 of the 11 fishless lakes sampled (all 8 were known to have been stocked with trout), but was absent from all fish-bearing lakes. This observation suggests that *Hesperodiaptomus* was able to recolonize these lakes, or emerge from resting eggs residing in the sediments after fish were eliminated. A number of other studies have shown strong negative effects of fish predation on large diaptomid species, including *Hesperodiaptomus* (Anderson 1980, Stoddard 1987, Donald et al. 2001), and recovery after fish introductions were stopped (Donald et al. 2001). In contrast, Parker et al. (2001) found that the congener *Hesperodiaptomus arcticus* was eliminated by introduced trout and did not return, even several years after trout had been removed from a northern Rocky Mountain lake, and suggested that the ability to recover from decades of fish predation was prevented by a lack of viable resting eggs within the lake sediments and poor ability to recolonize from other lakes. *Hesperodiaptomus kenai* distribution among LVNP lakes may be an indicator of the timing of fish population loss in previously stocked lakes, as this species may be slow to recover in lakes in which trout populations persisted for many years. Larvae of the predaceous phantom midge, *Chaoborus americanus*, and the large fairy shrimp, *Streptocephalus sealii*, were also only found in fishless lakes (*C. americanus* in 3 lakes, *S. sealii* in 1), further suggesting that large members of zooplankton/necton communities may have recovered following the loss of fish in some lakes.

In response to recommendations presented in what has come to be called the "Leopold Report", the National Park Service in 1972 adopted the policy that "no artificial stocking of fish will occur; artificial stocking of fish or fish eggs may only be employed to reestablish a native species. Naturally barren waters will not be stocked with either native or exotic fish species." The cessation of fish stocking has resulted in many historically-stocked, but originally fishless lakes to revert back to a fishless condition. A somewhat higher proportion of lakes within U. S. national parks are now fishless compared to public lands managed for a wider variety of human uses, including recreational fishing (Bahls 1992). In LVNP the policy to stop fish stocking has resulted in the majority of backcountry lakes reverting to their natural fishless, condition. In response, major components of aquatic communities appear to have recovered, or be on their way to recovery, from decades of fish predation. Strong fish effects will continue, however, in the few lakes that support self-sustaining fish populations and, in some cases provide popular recreational fisheries (e.g., Manzanita and Summit, and to a much less extent Butte, Snag and Horseshoe lakes).

This and the companion amphibian distribution study (Stead et al. 2005) were motivated in large part by the dramatic decline, and possible extinction of the Cascades frog (*Rana cascadae*) within LVNP and the surrounding region (e.g., Fellers and Drost 1993). Results of the amphibian distribution study clearly showed a negative association between fish and certain amphibian species within all lentic habitats suggesting that introduced fish may still play a role in determining the distribution of amphibians within the park and their recovery, not surprisingly, is much slower than that of littoral macroinvertebrates and zooplankton. Although fish are no longer present in most lakes, they are abundant in virtually all the major stream drainages within the park, so amphibians using these stream corridors to recolonize lentic habitats would have the run a gauntlet of fish predators. Even if stream-dwelling fishes slow recolonization rates, however, it is likely that a variety of other factors are playing stronger roles in limiting amphibian distribution, particularly *R. cascadae*, throughout the park (Fellers and Drost 1993, Stead et al.2005).

Literature Cited

Anderson, R. S. 1980. Relationship between trout and invertebrate species as predators and the structure of the crustacean and rotiferan plankton in mountain lakes. PP. 635-641 *in* Evolution and Ecology of Zooplankton Communities. University Press of New England, Hanover, NH.

Armstrong, T. W. and R. A. Knapp. 2004. Response by trout populations in alpine lakes to an experimental halt to stocking. Canadian Journal of Fisheries and Aquatic Sciences **61**: 2025-2037.

Bahls, P. 1992. The status of fish populations and management of high mountain lakes in the western United States. Northwest Science **66**: 183-193.

Bradford, D.F., S. D. Cooper, T.M. Jenkins, Jr., K. Kratz, O. Sarnelle, and A.D. Brown. 1998. Influences of natural acidity and introduced fish on faunal assemblages in California alpine lakes. Canadian Journal of Fisheries and Aquatic Sciences **55**: 2478-2491.

Brooks, J. L. and S. I. Dodson. 1965. Predation, body size and composition of plankton. Science **50**: 28-35.

Bull, E. L. and D. B. Marx. 2002. Influence of fish and habitat on amphibian communities in high elevation lakes in northeastern Oregon. Northwest Science **76**: 240-248.

Carlisle, D. M. and C. P. Hawkins. 1998. Relationships between invertebrate assemblage structure, 2 trout species, and habitat structure in Utah mountain lakes. Journal of the North American Benthological Society **17**: 286-300.

Carpenter, S. R. and J. F. Kitchell. 1993. The trophic cascade in lakes. Cambridge University Press.

Chess, D. W., F. Gibson, A. T. Scholz, and R. J. White. 1993. The introduction of Lahontan cutthroat trout into a previously fishless lake: feeding habits and effects upon the zooplankton and benthic community. Journal of Freshwater Ecology **8**: 215-225.

Clow, D. W., J. O. Sickman, R. G. Striegl, D. P. Krabbenhoft, J. G. Elliott, M. Dornblasser, D. A. Roth, and D. H. Campbell. 2003. Changes in the chemistry of lakes and precipitation in high-elevation national parks in the western United States, 1985-1999. Water Resources Research **39**(6): 1171-1184.

Dennison, A. 1977. Summary of 1976 lake survey data relating to the status of trout fisheries in Lassen Volcanic National Park.

Dill, W. A. and A. J. Cordone. 1997. History and status of introduced fishes in California, 1871-1996. California Department of Fish and Game. Fish Bulletin 178.

Donald, D. B. 1987. Assessment of the outcome of eight decades of trout stocking in the mountain national parks, Canada. North American Journal of Fisheries Management **7**: 545-553.

Donald, D. B., R. D. Vinebrooke, R. D., R. S. Anderson, J. Sytigiannis, and R. D. Graham. 2001. Recovery of zooplankton assemblages in mountain lakes from the effects of introduced sport fish. Canadian Journal of Fisheries and Aquatic Sciences **58**: 1822-1830.

Drake, D. C., and R. J. Naiman. 2000. An evaluation of restoration efforts in fishless lakes stocked with exotic trout. Conservation Biology **14**: 1807-1820.

Drost, C. 1991. Field Notes – September 14-22, 1991.

Dunham, J. B., D. S. Pilliod, and M. K. Young. 2004. Assessing the consequences of nonnative trout in headwater ecosystems in western North America. Fisheries **29**: 18-25.

Elser, J. J., C. Luecke, M. J. Brett, and C. R. Goldman. 1995. Effects of food web compensation after manipulation of rainbow trout in an oligotrophic lake. Ecology **76**: 52-69.

Fellers, G.M. and C.A. Drost. 1993. Disappearance of the cascade frog (*Rana cascadea*) at the southern end of its range, California, USA. Biological conservation **65**:177-181.

Haney, J. F. and D. J. Hall. 1973. Sugar-coated *Daphnia*: a preservation technique for Cladocera. Limnology and Oceanography **18**: 331-333.

Knapp, R.A. 1996. Non-native trout in natural lakes of the Sierra Nevada: an analysis of their distribution and impacts on native aquatic biota. In: Sierra Nevada ecosystem project: final report to Congress, volume III, assessments, commissioned reports and background information. Davis CA: Univ California. Wildland Resource Center Report **38**:363-407.

Knapp, R. A. 2005. Effects of nonnative fish and habitat characteristics on lentic herpetofauna in Yosemite National Park, USA. Biological Conservation **121**: 265-279.

Knapp, R. A., P. S. Corn, and D. E. Schindler. 2001a. The introduction of nonnative fish into wilderness lakes: good intentions, conflicting mandates, and unintended consequences. Ecosystems **4**: 275-278.

Knapp, R. A., K. R. Matthews, O. Sarnelle. 2001b. Resistance and resilience of alpine lake fauna to fish introductions. Ecological Monographs **71**: 301-421.

Lorenzen, C. J. 1967. Determination of chlorophyll and pheopigments: Spectrophotometric equations. Limnology and Oceanography **12**: 343-346.

Luecke, C. 1990. Changes in abundance and distribution of benthic macroinvertebrates after introduction of cutthroat trout in a previously fishless lake. Transactions of the American Fisheries Society **119**: 1010-1021.

Matthews, K. R., R. A. Knapp, and K. L. Pope. 2002. Garter snakes distributions in high elevation aquatic ecosystems: is there a link with declining amphibian populations? Journal of Herpetology **36**: 16-22.

Moyle, P. B. 2002. Inland fishes of California. University of California Press. Berkeley, CA.

National Park Service Water Resources Division. 1999. Baseline water quality data inventory and analysis: Lassen Volcanic National Park. Technical Report, NPS/NRWRD/NRTR-99/244.

Northcote, T. G., C. J. Walters, and J. M. B. Hume. 1978. Initial impacts of experimental fish introductions on the macro-zooplankton of small oligotrophic lakes. Verh. Internat. Verein. Limnol **20**: 2003-2012.

Parker, B. R., D. W. Schindler, D. B. Donald, and R. S. Anderson. 2001. The effects of stocking and removal of a nonnative salmonid on the plankton of an alpine lake. Ecosystems **4**: 334-345.

Pilliod, D. S. and C. R. Peterson. 2001. Local and landscape effects of introduced trout on amphibians in historically fishless watersheds. Ecosystems **4**: 322-333.

Pister, E. P. 2001. Wilderness fish stocking: history and perspective. Ecosystems **4**: 279-286.

Schindler, D. E., R. A. Knapp, R. A., and P. R. Leavitt. 2001. Alteration of nutrient cycles and algal production resulting from fish introductions into mountain lakes. Ecosystems **4**: 308-321

Stead, J. E., H. H. Welsh, Jr., and K. L. Pope. 2005. Census of amphibians and fishes in lentic habitats of Lassen Volcanic National Park: a report to the National Park Service. LAVO-00717.

Stoddard, J. L. 1987. Microcrustacean communities of high-elevation lakes in the Sierra Nevada, California. Journal of Plankton Research **9**: 631-650.

Wallis, O. L. 1977. Management of high-country lakes of California. Pages 53-64 *in* A. Hall R. May, editors. A symposium on the management of high mountain lakes in California's national parks. California Trout, Inc., San Francisco, CA.

Walters, C.J. and R.E. Vincent. 1973. Potential productivity of an alpine lake as indicated by removal and reintroduction of fish. Transactions of the America Fisheries Society **102**:675-697.

Wetzel, R. G. 2001. Limnology. Academic Press, London, UK.

Wissinger, S. A., A. R. McIntosh, and H. S. Greig. 2006. Impacts of introduced brown and rainbow trout on benthic invertebrate communities in shallow New Zealand lakes. Freshwater Biology **51**: 2009-2028.

NPS D-164, August 2008